M000047081

Presented To

_____

On the occasion of

_____

From

_____

Date

_____

Strong
AND
Courageous

© 1996 by Barbour and Company, Inc.

ISBN 1-55748-783-9

All rights reserved. No part of this publication may be reproduced or transmitted in any form or by any means without written permission of the publisher.

Unless otherwise noted, all scripture quotations are taken from the Holy Bible, King James Version.

Scripture quotations marked (NIV) are taken from the Holy Bible, New International Version®. NIV®. Copyright© 1973, 1978, 1984 by International Bible Society. Used by permission of Zondervan Publishing House. All rights reserved.

Member of the
Evangelical Christian
Publishers Association

Published by Barbour & Company, Inc.
P.O. Box 719
Uhrichsville, Ohio 44683

Printed in the United States of America.

Strong
AND
Courageous

WIT, WISDOM, AND INSPIRATION FOR THE MAN OF VISION

COMPILED BY E. CAUGHEY

A Barbour Book

Only be thou strong and very courageous,
that thou mayest observe to do according to all
the law . . . turn not from it to the right hand
or to the left, that thou mayest prosper
whithersoever thou goest.

JOSHUA — *Joshua 1:7*

■ ■ ■

Most men will proclaim every one his own
goodness: but a faithful man who can find?
Proverbs 20:6

■ ■ ■

This is courage in a man: to bear unflinchingly
what heaven sends.

EURIPIDES

Strong AND Courageous

Thou madest him [man] to have dominion over the works of thy hands; thou hast put all things under his feet . . . .

DAVID — *Psalm 8:6*

8

■ ■ ■

It is a wise father that knows his own child.

WILLIAM SHAKESPEARE

■ ■ ■

There is neither East nor West,
Border, nor Breed, nor Birth.
When two strong men stand face to face,
though they come from the ends
of the earth!

RUDYARD KIPLING

Remove not the ancient landmark, which
thy fathers have set.
Proverbs 22:28

■ ■ ■

One other thing stirs me when I look back
at my youthful days, the fact that so many people
gave me something or were something to me
without knowing it.
Albert Schweitzer

■ ■ ■

What thou art, that thou art; that God knoweth
thee to be and thou canst be said to be no greater.
Thomas à Kempis

■ ■ ■

Great men are they
who see
that the spiritual
is stronger
than any material force.

RALPH WALDO EMERSON

■ ■ ■

. . . The Lord seeth not as man seeth; for the
man looketh on the outward appearance, but the
Lord looketh on the heart.
1 Samuel 16:7b

■ ■ ■

Consider first, the great
or bright infers not excellence.
JOHN MILTON

■ ■ ■

Every blade of grass on earth whence it draws
its life, its strength; and so is man rooted to the
land from which he draws his faith together
with his life.
JOSEPH CONRAD

Strong AND Courageous

For thou shalt eat the labour of thine hands: happy shalt thou be, and it shall be well with thee.

Psalm 128:2

12

■ ■ ■

And God said, Let us make man in our image, after our likeness.

Genesis 1:26a

■ ■ ■

O Lord, let us not live to be useless, for Christ's sake.

JOHN WESLEY

W hat is man, that thou art mindful of him?. . .
For thou hast made him a little lower then
the angels, and hast crowned him with glory
and honour.
Psalm 8:4-5

■ ■ ■

I n God have I put my trust: I will not be afraid
what man can do unto me.
Psalm 56:11

■ ■ ■

T he care of God for us is a great thing if a man
believe it at the heart: it plucks the burden
of sorrow from him.
EURIPIDES

Strong
AND Courageous

■ ■ ■

T he just man
walketh in his integrity:
his children
are blessed after him.

Proverbs 20:7

■ ■ ■

There is nothing nobler or more admirable than
when two people who see eye to eye keep house
as man and wife, confounding their enemies
and delighting their friends.

HOMER (9TH CENTURY B.C.)

■ ■ ■

This is what a father ought to be about:
helping his son to form the habit of doing right
on his own initiative, rather than because he is
afraid of some serious consequence.

TERENCE (160 B.C.)

■ ■ ■

Lo, children are an heritage of the Lord:
and the fruit if the womb is his reward.

Psalm 127:3

Strong **AND** **Courageous**

16

Lord, give us faith that right makes might,
and in that faith let us to the end dare to do
our duty as we understand it.

ABRAHAM LINCOLN

■ ■ ■

He hath shewed thee, O man, what is good;
and what doth the Lord require of thee,
but to do justly, and to love mercy, and to
walk humbly with thy God?

Micah 6:8

■ ■ ■

Render to Caesar the things that are Caesar's,
and to God the things that are God's . . . .

JESUS — *Mark 12:17*

Above all, my brothers, do not swear—
not by heaven or by earth or by anything else.
Let your "Yes" be yes,
and your "No," no . . . .
James 5:12 (NIV)

■ ■ ■

There is a destiny which makes us brothers;
None goes his way alone.
EDWIN MARKHAM

■ ■ ■

Have we not all one father?
hath not one God created us?
Malachi 2:10

■ ■ ■

A new commandment
I give unto you,
That ye love one another . . . .
By this shall all men
know that ye are my disciples,
If ye have love
one to another.

JESUS — *John 13:34-35*

■ ■ ■

My words fly up, my thoughts remain below.
Words without thoughts never to heaven go.
WILLIAM SHAKESPEARE

■ ■ ■

For who makes you different
from anyone else?
What do you have that you
did not receive?
PAUL — *1 Corinthians 4:7* (NIV)

■ ■ ■

Who of you by worrying can add
a single hour to his life?
Matthew 6:27 (NIV)

Strong AND **Courageous**

The woods would be very silent
if no birds sang
except those who sang best.
HENRY DAVID THOREAU

■ ■ ■

Life is one long process of getting tired.
SAMUEL BUTLER

■ ■ ■

Marriage should be honored by all, and the
marriage bed kept pure, for God will judge the
adulterer and all the sexually immoral.
Hebrews 13:4 (NIV)

No man has ever lived that had enough,
Of children's gratitude or woman's love.
WILLIAM BUTLER YEATS

■ ■ ■

"But while he was still a long way off,
his father saw him and was filled
with compassion for him;
he ran to his son, threw his arms around him
and kissed him."
Luke 15:20 (NIV)

■ ■ ■

"How much more valuable is a man than
a sheep! Therefore it is lawful to do good
on the Sabbath."
JESUS — *Matthew 12:12* (NIV)

Strong
AND
Courageous

22

■ ■ ■

Open thy mouth,
judge righteously,
and plead the cause
of the poor and needy.

Proverbs 31:9

■ ■ ■

I am greater than the stars for I know that they
are up there and they do not know
that I am down here.
WILLIAM TEMPLE

■ ■ ■

I count life just a stuff
to try the soul's strength on.
ROBERT BROWNING

■ ■ ■

The race is not to the swift or the battle to the
strong, nor does food come to the wise
or wealth to the brilliant or favor to the learned;
but time and chance happen to them all.
Ecclesiastes 9:11 (NIV)

Strong AND Courageous

24

The glory of young men is their strength:
and the beauty of old men is the gray head.
Proverbs 20:29

■ ■ ■

God is the brave man's hope,
and not the coward's excuse.
Plutarch

■ ■ ■

Blessed is the man who perseveres under trial,
because when he has stood the test, he will
receive the crown of life that God has promised
to those who love him.
James 1:12 (NIV)

Two men please God—who serves him
with all his heart because he knows him;
who seeks him with all his heart
because he knows him not.

NIKITA IVANOVICH PANIN

■ ■ ■

An honest man's the noblest work of God.

ALEXANDER POPE

■ ■ ■

Blessed is the man unto whom the Lord
imputeth not iniquity, and in whose spirit
there is no guile.

Psalm 32:2

Strong AND Courageous

■ ■ ■

A man must thank his
defects, and stand
in some terror of his talents.

RALPH WALDO EMERSON

■ ■ ■

And when youth's gone
    As men count going, twixt us two alone
Still let me be
Thy little child, left learning at Thy knee.

ANONYMOUS

■ ■ ■

He who has daughters is always a shepherd.

Spanish proverb

■ ■ ■

That our sons may be as plants grown up in
their youth; that our daughters may be as corner
stones, polished after the similitude of a palace
. . . yea, happy is that people whose
God is the Lord.

Psalm 144:12, 15b

Strong AND Courageous

28

Adversity reminds men of religion.

LIVY

■ ■ ■

Blessed is the man that walketh not
in the counsel of the ungodly,
nor standeth in the way of sinners,
nor sitteth in the seat of the scornful.
But his delight is in the law of the Lord;
and in his law doth he meditate day and night.

Psalm 1:1-2

■ ■ ■

One on God's side is a majority.

WENDELL PHILLIPS

Courage is resistance to fear, mastery of fear—
not absence of fear.

MARK TWAIN

■ ■ ■

No man is an island.

JOHN DONNE

■ ■ ■

And yet I am as strong this day as I was
in the day that Moses sent me: as my strength
was then, even so is my strength now, for war,
both to go out, and to come in.

CALEB — *Joshua 14:11*

■ ■ ■

Husbands,
love your wives,
just as Christ
loved
the church
and gave himself up
for her.

PAUL—*Ephesians 5:25* (NIV)

■ ■ ■

And Samuel grew, and the Lord was with him, and did let none of his words fall to the ground.
1 Samuel 3:19

■ ■ ■

If a man die, shall he live again? all the days of my appointed time will I wait, till my change come.
Job— *Job 14:14*

■ ■ ■

Endure hardship as discipline; God is treating you as sons. For what son is not disciplined by his father?
Hebrews 12:7 (NIV)

Strong AND Courageous

32

I have never been able to conceive
mankind without him.

F. DOSTOEVSKY

■ ■ ■

"What good will it be for a man if he gains
the whole world, yet forfeits his soul?"
JESUS — *Matthew 16:26* (NIV)

■ ■ ■

. . . Then Peter remembered the word
the Lord had spoken to him:
"Before the rooster crows today,
you will disown me three times."
And he went outside and wept bitterly.
Luke 22:61-62 (NIV)

Chasten thy son while there is hope,
and let not thy soul spare for his crying.
Proverbs 19:18

■ ■ ■

"I baptize with water . . . but among you
stands one you do not know. He is the one
who comes after me, the thongs of
whose sandals I am not worthy to untie."
JOHN THE BAPTIST — *John 1:26-27* (NIV)

■ ■ ■

Verily, verily, I say unto thee,
Except a man be born again, he cannot
see the kingdom of God.
JESUS — *John 3:3*

■ ■ ■

Always do right.
This will gratify
some people,
and astonish the rest.

MARK TWAIN

■ ■ ■

Unless the Lord builds the house,
its builders labor in vain.
Psalm 127:1a (NIV)

■ ■ ■

Therefore shall a man leave his father and
his mother, and shall cleave unto his wife:
and they shall be one flesh.
Genesis 2:24

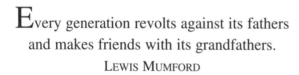

Every generation revolts against its fathers
and makes friends with its grandfathers.
LEWIS MUMFORD

Strong AND Courageous

36

. . . O my son Absalom, my son,
my son Absalom! would God I had died
for thee . . . .

DAVID — *2 Samuel 18:33*

■ ■ ■

It's not a man's great frame
Or breadth of shoulders makes his manhood
count:
A man of sense has always the advantage.

SOPHOCLES

■ ■ ■

A wise man is strong; yea, a man of
knowledge increaseth strength.

Proverbs 24:5

Be it ever so humble, there's no place like home for wearing what you like.

GEORGE ADE

■ ■ ■

We are things of a day.
What are we?
What are we not?
The shadow of a dream
is man, no more.

PINDAR

■ ■ ■

Let no man deceive himself. If any man among you seemeth to be wise in this world, let him become a fool, that he may be wise.

PAUL—*1 Corinthians 3:18*

■ ■ ■

He that is faithful
in that which is least
is faithful also in much;
and he
that is unjust in the least
is unjust also in much.

Jesus — *Luke 16:10*

■ ■ ■

P raise the Lord with harp. . . . Sing unto him
a new song; play skilfully with a loud noise.
Psalm 33:2-3

■ ■ ■

A nd David danced before the Lord
with all his might . . . .
2 Samuel 6:14

■ ■ ■

A man cannot be said to succeed in this life
who does not satisfy one friend.
HENRY DAVID THOREAU

Strong AND Courageous

40

But Noah found grace in the eyes of the Lord.
Genesis 6:8

■ ■ ■

. . . The Lord be between me and thee, and
between my seed and thy seed for ever . . . .
JONATHAN — *1 Samuel 20:42*

■ ■ ■

Remember not the sins of my youth,
nor my transgressions:
according to thy mercy remember thou me
for thy goodness' sake, O Lord.
Psalms 25:7

The child is father of the man.
WILLIAM WORDSWORTH

■ ■ ■

Art thou the first man that was born?
or wast thou made before the hills?
Hast thou heard the secret
of God? and dost thou restrain wisdom
to thyself?
Job 15:7-8

■ ■ ■

I know that everything God does
will endure forever; nothing can be added
to it and nothing taken from it. God does
it so that men will revere him.
Ecclesiastes 3:14 (NIV)

■ ■ ■

T here is no more lovely,
friendly and charming
relationship, communion
or company
than a good marriage.

MARTIN LUTHER

■ ■ ■

Few things are harder to put up with than
the annoyance of a good example.
MARK TWAIN

■ ■ ■

The Bible was written for men with a head
upon their shoulders.
MARTIN LUTHER

■ ■ ■

You have made my days
a mere handbreadth; the span of my years
is as nothing before you. Each man's life
is but a breath.
Psalm 39:5 (NIV)

Strong **AND** **Courageous**

Man that is in honour, and understandeth not,
is like the beasts that perish.
Psalm 49:20

44

■ ■ ■

I have fought the good fight, I have finished the
race, I have kept the faith.
PAUL — *2 Timothy 4:7* (NIV)

■ ■ ■

This is no time for ease and comfort.
It is time to dare and endure.
WINSTON CHURCHILL

Test everything. Hold on to the good.
PAUL — *1 Thessalonians 5:21* (NIV)

■ ■ ■

Mark the perfect man, and behold the upright:
for the end of that man is peace.
Psalm 37:37

■ ■ ■

. . . Choose you this day whom ye will serve;
. . . but as for me and my house,
we will serve the Lord.
JOSHUA — *Joshua 24:15*

■ ■ ■

B lessed is the man
unto whom the Lord
imputeth not iniquity,
and in whose spirit
there is no guile.

Psalm 32:2

■ ■ ■

I hate the giving of the hand unless
the whole man accompanies it.
RALPH WALDO EMERSON

■ ■ ■

An honest heart being the first blessing,
a knowing head is the second.
THOMAS JEFFERSON

■ ■ ■

As he that fears God fears nothing else,
so, he that sees God sees everything else.
JOHN DONNE

Strong AND Courageous

48

And the Lord God formed man
of the dust of the ground,
and breathed into his nostrils
the breath of life;
and man became a living soul.
Genesis 2:7

■ ■ ■

A good man obtaineth favour of the Lord:
but a man of wicked devices will he condemn.
Proverbs 12:2

■ ■ ■

... Fear God and keep his commandments,
for this is the whole duty of man.
Ecclesiates 12:13b (NIV)

The awareness of our own strength
makes us modest.
PAUL CÉZANNE

■ ■ ■

That is why, for Christ's sake, I delight
in weaknesses, in insults, in hardships,
in persecutions, in difficulties.
For when I am weak,
then I am strong.
PAUL — *2 Corinthians 12:10* (NIV)

■ ■ ■

A fool uttereth all his mind; but a wise man
keepeth it in till afterwards.
Proverbs 29:11

■ ■ ■

If God is for us, who can be against us?

PAUL—*Romans 8:31* (NIV)

■ ■ ■

"For by your words you will be acquitted, and by your words you will be condemned."
JESUS — *Matthew 12:37* (NIV)

■ ■ ■

"... Anyone who does not take up his cross
and follow me is not worthy of me.
Whoever finds his life will lose it,
and whoever loses his life for my sake
will find it."
JESUS — *Matthew 10:38-39* (NIV)

■ ■ ■

If you don't crack the shell,
you can't eat the nut.
Russian proverb

Strong AND Courageous

I can do everything through him
who gives me strength.
PAUL — *Philippians 4:13* (NIV)

■ ■ ■

We know what we are, but know not
what we may be.
William Shakespeare

■ ■ ■

The spirit of man is the candle of the Lord,
searching all the inward parts of the belly.
Proverbs 20:27

Anyone who claims to be in the light but hates his brother is still in the darkness.
1 John 2:9 (NIV)

■ ■ ■

You shall judge of a man by his foes as well as his friends.
JOSEPH CONRAD

■ ■ ■

"Nazareth! Can anything good come from there?"
NATHANEAL — *John 1:46* (NIV)

■ ■ ■

For God did not give us
a spirit of timidity,
but a spirit of power,
of love and
of self-discipline.

PAUL—*2 Timothy 1:7* (NIV)

■ ■ ■

Fortune, thou hadst no deity, if men
Had wisdom.

BEN JONSON

■ ■ ■

I don't like work—no man does—
but I like what is in work—
the chance to find yourself.
Your own reality—
for yourself, not for others—
what no other man can ever know.

JOSEPH CONRAD

■ ■ ■

When my friends are one-eyed,
I look at them in profile.

JOSEPH JOUBERT

Strong AND Courageous

Man's goings are of the Lord:
how can a man then understand
his own way?
Proverbs 20:24

■ ■ ■

When I was a child, I spake as a child…
I thought as a child: but when I became a man,
I put away childish things.
PAUL — *1 Corinthians 13:11*

■ ■ ■

Anyone can be heroic from time to time,
but a gentleman is something you have to be
all the time. Which isn't easy.
LUIGI PIRANDELLO

A round man cannot be expected to fit
in a square hole right away.
He must have time
to modify his shape.
MARK TWAIN

■ ■ ■

M en are slower to recognize blessings
than evils.
LIVY

■ ■ ■

H ow often we find ourselves turning our backs
on our actual friends, that we may go and
meet their ideal cousins.
HENRY DAVID THOREAU

Strong AND Courageous

■ ■ ■

"Whoever acknowledges
me before men,
I will also acknowledge him
before my father
in heaven."

JESUS — *Matthew 10:32* (NIV)

■ ■ ■

Only the wearer knows where the shoe pinches.
English proverb

■ ■ ■

He that can't endure the bad,
will not live to see the good.
Yiddish proverb

■ ■ ■

Endure hardship with us like a good soldier
of Christ Jesus.
PAUL — *2 Timothy 2:3* (NIV)

Strong
AND
Courageous

60

"When I lie down I think,
'How long before I get up'?"
Job 7:4a (NIV)

■ ■ ■

Blessed is the man whom thou chastenest,
O Lord, and teachest him out of thy law.
Psalm 94:12

■ ■ ■

It is enough; Joseph my son is yet alive:
I will go and see him before I die.
Jacob — *Genesis 45:28*

W hat man is he that feareth the Lord? him
shall he teach in the way that he shall choose.
Psalm 25:12

■ ■ ■

V alor is a gift.
Those having it never know for sure
whether they have it till the test comes.
And those having it in one test never know for
sure if they will have it when the next test comes.
CARL SANDBURG

■ ■ ■

M en are not prisoners of fate,
but only prisoners of their own minds.
FRANKLIN DELANO ROOSEVELT

■ ■ ■

I hope I shall always
possess firmness and virtue
enough to maintain what I
consider the most enviable
of all titles,
the character of
an "Honest Man."

GEORGE WASHINGTON

■ ■ ■

T o thine own self be true,
And it must follow, as the night the day,
Thou canst not then be false to any man.
WILLIAM SHAKESPEARE

63

■ ■ ■

I will not rule over you,
neither shall my son rule over you:
the Lord shall rule over you.
GIDEON — *Judges 8:23*

■ ■ ■

W hat we seek we shall find;
what we flee from flees from us.
RALPH WALDO EMERSON

Strong AND **Courageous**

64

One man with courage makes a majority.
ANDREW JACKSON

■ ■ ■

Fathers, do not exasperate your children;
instead, bring them up in the training
and instruction of the Lord.
PAUL—*Ephesians 6:4* (NIV)

■ ■ ■

Finally, brothers, whatever is true,
whatever is noble, whatever is right,
whatever is pure, whatever is lovely,
whatever is admirable—
if anything is excellent or praiseworthy—
think about such things.
PAUL — *Philippians 4:8* (NIV)